Contents

INTRODUCTION

Business plans are probably the element of a business' growth with the most misconceptions. Most entrepreneurs believe, wrongly so, that business plans are helpful only for startup business ventures – *that's not true*.

Whether you're running a coffee shop at the end of the street or starting a high-end fashion clothing line, the fact that these endeavors would require significant amount of money, time, and other resources call for the need of a robust business plan.

The plan for each business obviously would be different but it shall serve the same purpose – *providing a direction*.

Startup Businesses

For startup businesses, a business plan entails the goals of the new company, the processes and strategies it would implement to achieve these goals, the founders of the company, and most importantly, why each of them is the right person for their designated posts. This plan would also detail out the initial capital required to get the business going and fuel the preliminary growth that may lead to profitability in the future.

Established Businesses

The business plans for existing businesses slightly differ from the ones made for startup ventures. These business plans are more focused on capitalizing the company's competitive advantage that powers rapid growth and better innovation. A business plan for existing businesses is not an inert document; rather, it takes the form of active tools used to track and promote business growth and identify significant drawbacks that may derail the progress of a business.

For anyone who takes their business seriously, a business plan is a substantial tool contributing to the collective success of their business.

WHAT IS A BUSINESS PLAN?

To keep it simple, a business plan is a road map that decides the future course of a business.

It could be something as simple as a small description of business strategy scribbled on a paper, but in most cases, a business plan is a detailed written document that outlines and helps businesses set goals and devise appropriate strategies to achieve them.

They may start as a simple concept, but at some point business plans germinate into inherently strategic documents.

Right here, right now, you have a certain set of abilities and resources. In the near future, let's say in about five years, you want to see your business with a different set of abilities and resources, with increased assets and profitability.

Your business plan will show how you plan to get from here to where you wish to see your business in 5 years' time.

WHY DO YOU NEED A BUSINESS PLAN?

The most clichéd responses to this question would be for *"applying for a business loan"* or *"starting a business"*, but as we have already established – business plans are a lot more than just that. They can lay down the foundations of a new business as effectively as they can help a running business stay on track with its plans and opportunities.

Each business has its own set of short-term and long-term goals. These may include short-term sales targets, growth in assets and profitability in the long run, and so on. A business plan covers all of these aspects. Hence, there could be various reasons for drawing up a business plan. We are listing down the most prominent ones down here for you.

1. ***It gives you a game plan.*** To achieve a goal, be it short term or long term, it is important to have a strategy that is properly executed. This calls for establishing goals, setting priorities, and measuring performance overtime. It gives rise to questions like *"Will our product and pricing strategy attract our target customers?"*, *"Does our product have the features that customers want?"*, *"Will setting up a new plant contribute to the overall profitability of the company"*, or *"Should the company invest in Project A or Project B?"* A business plan addresses all these things in greater detail with possible solutions.

2. ***It streamlines individual goals into a collective one.*** Normally companies are not being run by a single person. There are partners, managers, and then the employees that put in combined efforts to run the business. Each person may have their own personal goals that might not necessarily be in coherence with the company's goals, unless there is an effective business plan that ensures everyone in the company is on the same page when it comes to accomplishing goals.

3. ***It ensures emotional stability.*** There are countless instances in a business where the situation gets absolutely manic. There will be passion to pursue your goals; there will be moments of

doubt, the fear of failing, and fatigue. These emotions can easily overpower your ability of making the right decisions. This is the time where you can take a step back, go through your business plan, realign your efforts, and work towards the proper execution of the plan.

4. *It helps raise capital.* Whether you're running a small business, are looking to expand your current operations, or starting out on a new business venture, you will need finance. If you wish to borrow or raise finance for your business, you need to provide the potential investors with a compelling vision of your business that convinces them to invest. A business plan – a good one can help you communicate just that.

5. *It prevents substantial mistakes.* It is always better to check the depth of water before taking a plunge into it. This proves true for businesses too. Business plans are formulated after thorough research. They provide a detailed insight into business aspects that may or may not work for the company. In addition to that, these plans require constant updating according to the changing business conditions. This makes sure that the company stays on the right track with minimal chances of business blunders.

Apart from these, a business plan can be used for various other reasons that may include setting benchmarks, predicting future market trends, exploring new market niches or general accountability. It's a versatile tool that can help set a track for any business.

MAKING A BUSINESS PLAN

A business plan may be able to serve multiple purposes for a business, but it is only effective if it is properly put together. A successful business plan needs to follow a set of guidelines generally accepted for both its content and form. Primarily, there are three parts a business plan is divided into. These cover:

- **The business concept section:** This is where the business plan details out everything about the business. It discusses the structure of the business, the industry it operates in, the products and/or services it offers, and the basic plan for the business' success.
- **The market section:** This section concentrates on the potential customers. The market segment the business is targeting, the factors that influence their buying behavior and power, why they buy the company's products, etc. Also included in this section is an analysis of the market competition faced by the company and how it plans to combat that for greater market share.
- **The financial section:** This section is all about the money. It would include budgets, cash flow statements, revenues and expenditure, financing options, financial ratios, and financial statements. It is needless to say that this part of the business plan would require a lot of attention and possibly the help of a professional accountant or an expert to be completed.

Now that you are familiar with what a business plan is and how it works, it is time to move on to the greater task of drafting one. There is a lot of effort, hard work, research and calculation that goes into the compilation of a successful business plan, so we have broken down the process into ten steps. Over the chapters that follow, you will learn about what to include and what not to include in a business plan, and the elements that make it effective.

STEP 1: DETERMINE YOUR BUSINESS GOALS

First things first; you can't begin developing a business plan unless you have a clear objective for it. We mentioned earlier that a business plan is a roadmap – *to where?* – To the collective goal of the organization.

Every business can have a different goal that it wishes to achieve. These goals can sprout from various sources like customer expectations, shareholder demands, employee satisfaction, need of the hour, and so on.

The important thing to consider here is the fact that it is almost impossible to work towards multiple goals at the same time. The smart way about it is to determine a long term goal that the business wishes to achieve *(consistent growth)* and then break down the process into smaller achievable targets that work towards the accomplishment of the final goal.

Setting goals help you devise a comprehensive strategy to reach them. Determining goals often does not come easy –but it's not entirely impossible. Let's suppose your ultimate goal is to introduce a new product into the market.

Ask yourself the following questions:

- Is the product unique or does it already exists in the market?
- Do you have a competitive advantage *(what sets your product apart?)*?
- Are there any shortcomings that you might need to overcome?
- What is the preferred timeline?
- What pricing strategy would you implement? Would that be enough to earn you the desired profit margin?
- What do you need to do in order to keep the operating costs low enough to ensure a profit?
- How do you plan to acquire the said product? Would you manufacture it, assemble it, or distribute it?

Once you answer these questions, you will have a set of new goals that you need to work on in order to achieve the final goal of a profitable launch of your new product. As a next step:

- You need to first distinguish between your long term and short term goals.
- Prioritize your goals in terms of importance and expected time frames.
- Align your short term goals into stepping stones leading to your eventual long term goal.

It is important to remember that each goal on your list would require a separate business plan; unless they are goals that are collateral to each other. For example, a plan to increase the level of *customer satisfaction* can in due course lead to a *higher market share* for your company.

Objectives don't just layout the foundations of a business plan; they also help you identify the important roles required to achieve them. They help define the ideal roles of stakeholders – the employees, the contractors, the management, the owners, the consultants, and the customers – that can boost the company's journey towards the accomplishment of its goals.

Your goals will make sure you have a clear sight of what you wish your business to achieve. An extremely crucial consideration at this point is to make sure the objectives you determine are realistic and obtainable. Aiming for an IPO within 6 months of starting business is certainly not pragmatic.

STEP 2: RECOGNIZE THE STRENGTHS OF YOUR BUSINESS

Whether they express it or not, business management/owners are looking for sustainable growth of the business. *How much should we grow in the upcoming quarter? Can we afford expanding into a new market segment? Should we expand our operations at this point?*

It's true; business growth does not come overnight. It's a structure that needs to be built brick by brick in order to make sure the growth attained is reliable and sustainable. Continuing the same example, we used in *Step 1: Determine Your Business Goals*, the introduction of a new product into the market will too, eventually lead to business growth.

To achieve these goals, businesses need to take a capabilities-driven approach when formulating a strategy. For that purpose, you need to identify the strengths of your business. To begin with, try to find comprehensive answers for:

- *Why do customers prefer our product/service over the competitors'?* The answer to this question could be the distinct traits of your product, the quality of your after-sale services, or even the pricing strategies you implement. Take the time to survey the possibilities; you'd be surprised at the reasons that pop up.
- *How are we different and possibly better?* Another important player in achieving long-term growth is the market share you have. When you put your product out in the market, in most cases you're not the only one selling it – there's competition too. This is where your individual capability as a company comes under the limelight. You need to have a competitive advantage to gain a better market share – and that competitive advantage is just another strength you possess.

What's important to note here is the fact that not all business strengths are connected to the market. It is in fact the in-house strengths that can actually change the course of a business' quest for sustainable growth. The companies that actually achieve lasting success are the ones that let their capabilities drive their directives.

Your company's strengths may include:

- A potent management with strong leadership abilities
- Professional staff with relevant expertise and experience
- Powerful marketing strategy and product differentiation
- Competent forecasting and diagnosing of problems and weaknesses
- Adequate finance to support intended growth
- Low turnover of employees
- Healthy cash flows

Basically, anything that helps promote the projected goals of the company can and should qualify as strength.

The objective of identifying the business' strengths is to enable you to plot a goal course that you can build your success on. However, identifying the strengths alone will not suffice. Every business has its weaknesses – you need to recognize and eliminate them. There would be threats; keep a look out for them and take timely measures to overcome them. When the opportunities arise, be prepared to properly capitalize on them.

Why are we discussing all this? Because you can't have an effective business plan unless you know what cards to play, which ones to avoid, and which ones could get the win for you.

Step 3: Know Your Market

A strong business plan requires a thorough knowledge of the business' potential customer. If you don't know who you would be selling to, or who would be buying your product/service; nothing you take forward from there will make any sense.

Whether you're planning expansion or looking to start a new business, you need a market to sell your product/service to. A cliché list of questions can help you determine the regulatory market trends that can impact the plans you have for your business. These questions may include:

- Who buys your product?
- Why do they buy your product?
- What do they gain by spending on your product?

However, when it comes to identifying the target market, you need to dig deeper for a reliable analysis. Here's how you can identify your target customers:

Identify the Needs/Problems You're Providing Solution For
When you begin a business venture, you need to have an idea. This idea has to be a possible solution for a problem faced by the community in general. The foremost step in identifying your target market is to determine the problems you would be addressing.

Who's Your Customer?
The next step is to shortlist all the people who might be suffering from the problem you're providing a solution for. If you're a business selling organic soaps, these people might include:

- Those suffering from skin diseases
- Those with sensitive skins
- Those who prefer organic products over other

The list may further divide into age groups and genders, for further analysis.

Who Will Likely Gain Value from What You're Offering?
Here you need to determine who would reap the most benefit from your product/service. You need to find answers for:

- Who finds these problems most irritable?
- Who stands to lose out the most by not using your product?

Following our example, these people would include the ones suffering from skin diseases or the ones who have sensitive skins. This will help you capitalize on these problems, and come up with a plan that is compelling enough to attract the customer base you wish to target.

What is Your Company About?
Once you have the target market, you need to evaluate your ability as a company. Do you have the expertise to deliver what you will be committing to deliver? Do your knowledge, location, and other factors support your business plan?

At this stage, it is important to assess every single factor that does or does not work in your favor. Since our initial example pertained to the launch of a new product/service, favoring factors can include the uniqueness of your product, your geographical location as a business, the company's standing in the industry, and everything else that ideally makes your target market flock to your product.

In the same scenario, if we change the final objective, everything discussed under this particular heading would consequently need alteration as well.

STEP 4: THE EXECUTIVE SUMMARY

With the nitty-gritty done and dusted with, it is now time to move to the more important aspects of the business plan. Every business plan begins with an *executive summary*.

An executive summary is rightfully declared as the most vital element of the business plan. It summarizes the complete vision behind the plan into a detailed explanation of:

- Where the company stands today
- Where do you wish to see it in the future?
- The business idea *(subject matter of the business plan)* and how will it be successful

The executive summary is what defines the rest of your business plan. It is what you need to grab the interest of the board of directors for approval or to prove to the investors that your plan is worth investing *(in case you're looking to raise finance)*.

You obviously can't impress the reader unless you emphasize on the potency of your plan – this is where you put to use the information gathered in *Step 2: Recognize the Strengths of Your Business* and *Step 3: Know Your Market.*

The essentials of a comprehensive executive summary include:

For a Startup Venture
If you have only just started your business, you obviously wouldn't have the amount of detail about the company as an established firm would. So that part should be covered with your entrepreneurial/industry experience, background, and the areas you wish to focus on. It should also include the decisions that led you to start this venture.

You need to exhibit the meticulous market analysis you've conducted, the market you wish to target, the market gaps that your product/services can fill and how.

You should aim to convince the readers that your plan is *the* road to success.

For Existing Businesses
Existing businesses need to mention the following information:

- **Your Mission Statement**: A paragraph describing what is your business all about – its values, operations, and aspirations.
- **Company Description**: A concise statement that reveals the date of company formation, its founders, their roles, the number of employees, and the business location(s).
- **Growth Trajectory**: A highlight of your business growth. This could include: an increase in share prices or a continuous rise in annual profits
- **Your Products/Services**: Include a brief description of the products/services you offer.
- **Financial Details**: For the purpose of the executive summary, you only need to summarize the details of your current investors and banks.
- **The Future Plans**: This is your long-term vision/vision statement – where do you wish to take your company.

You need to realize that everything mentioned in the executive summary, except the mission statement, would be discussed in depth later in the plan – *so keep it concise!* It's best to limit the executive summary to one page, and making every word count.

The executive summary may be the very first section of your business plan, but it is always written in the end. *Why? Because it needs to highlight the components of your plan that make it feasible and possibly profitable in the future!*

That leaves you to work on the second element *(The Business Overview)* first, which we've covered in the next chapter as Step 5.

STEP 5: THE BUSINESS OVERVIEW

The actual second stage of the business plan is an overview of the business. Your plan at this point should outline what your business offers or is planning to offer and the strategies and methods you wish to make use of in order to sell what you offer.

It is crucial that the business overview you write is top-notch and includes everything that needs to be included. You need to stay focused, concise, and to the point as you take the time to effectively describe your business for the intended readers.

There is no hard and fast rule as to how long the business overview should be. It could vary anywhere between a few paragraphs and several pages, as long as it entails the details of your business.

Normally, the following things are included in a business overview:

1. Basic Data
This will include the name of the business, the structure *(partnership, corporation, or proprietorship),* the name of the owners, and the location of the company. Also, you need to identify which classification your business falls into – wholesale, retail, manufacturing, or service.

2. The History
Where you started, the background of the business, how did you come up with the concept of your business, and when you started – it should be a brief insight into the drive behind your venture.

3. The Mission Statement
The mission statement is the concept and purpose behind your business.

4. Business Dynamics
This section should include the relevant information about the industry you operate in, the current atmosphere of the business, and the future business-improving opportunities that may arise in the.

5. The Business Idea Behind the Plan

Remember we were launching a new product/service? That's your business idea. Give a description of your product/service and the competitive advantage you enjoy over other comparable products/services in the industry.

6. The Goals

The goals we initially discussed in *Step1: Determine Your Business Goals*, list them down here – both short and long term goals that you wish to achieve through this business plan/idea.

For example, a short term goal could be getting the prototype of your new product approved and having it distributed across the globe in say about a decade's time could be the long term goal.

Once you're done with drafting a detailed overview of the company, you need to move to the next step in the business – *The Marketing Plan*

STEP 6: THE MARKETING PLAN

You've got a fantastic product – that's great! But it wouldn't sell until the relevant customers know about it. This is where a marketing plan comes into action.

Most people mistake marketing to be solely advertising – *it's not!* Marketing is a much wider subject that includes everything from the promotional goods, advertising to public relations. Money spent on effective marketing allows the business to reap a return.

Hence, a business plan without a marketing plan is more or less useless. There are some basic steps for creating a marketing plan. These include:

1. ***The Target Market.*** Refer to *Step 3: Know Your Market* and determine what you need to do in order to reach out to your potential customers.

2. ***Evaluate your competition.*** To make sure your marketing plan is nothing like that of your competitor's, you need to gain adequate knowledge of whom you're competing with. This does not just cover the products/services they offer. It includes their marketing strategies, their USP (Unique Selling Proposition), their distribution channels, their strengths and weaknesses. Evaluating competition is discussed in more detail in the next chapter *Step 7: Size Up Your Competition – Competitive Analysis.*

3. ***Consider your brand.*** If you already have an established brand, it will have an impact on the way customers perceive your products/services. In this case, your marketing strategy should make effective use of your brand, reinforcing it wherever possible to boost sales and revenues. You need to have a clear picture of what your marketing policy should reflect about your business.

4. ***Capitalize on the benefits.*** When designing your marketing strategy, you need to keep in mind that you need to properly

highlight the benefits your product/service is providing to the clients - the problems they solve. Customers don't buy a product, they rather spend on the solutions and benefits attached to these products. Your marketing plan should be more about what the customers receive, instead of what you provide.

5. ***Don't forget to differentiate.*** *How do you make your product stand out from similar products in the market?* You try something different! This could be in terms of properties, design, packaging, price, or even the uniqueness of ingredients.

Another important thing that needs to be considered when designing a marketing strategy is the marketing budget – the amount of money you are willing to spend on your promotional activities. Budgets can vary from company to company and are therefore clearly a matter of choice and financial capability.

When you iron out the above mentioned aspects, the marketing plan section in your business plan would look something like:

The Market
How you could figure out the target market has already been discussed in ***Step 3: Know Your Market.*** The target market for Organic Soaps can be Washington, Oregon, Idaho, Wyoming, and other US states with high skin cancer statistics. It can be further simplified into the potential client base being men over 50 – they are more prone to contract skin cancer.

The Strategy
Following our example of launching organic soaps, a comprehensive marketing strategy could be centered on three basic initiatives:

- ***Web Initiatives.*** The company's social media platforms and website can be used to attract the potential clients to the possible benefits of using the soap. Use engaging online content and promote the product on related web pages.

- **Indirect Promotion.** You could partner with local dermatologists and oncologists to help you promote your product by prescribing it to their patients.
- **Promotional Events.** Skin cancer drives, cancer awareness weeks, seminars focusing on your target market can help you draw crowds to buy your products.

The Price

Whether you wish to charge a premium price for your product/service or launch it at a discounted price, this is where you decide how much your customers should pay for the solutions you're providing them.

Companies use various pricing strategies to penetrate a market and gain a considerable share of it. How you plan to capture your market is entirely up to you.

The Distribution

There's always the extremely important question looming over the head when you're making a marketing plan:

How will my product reach my customers?

Do you plan to sell online, partner with established distributors, or open a proper outlet for your brand?

Throughout the process, the key is to understand your market and how you plan to reach out to it. You should be able to explain in this section how you plan to attract your customers and make them stay.

STEP 7: SIZE UP YOUR COMPETITION – COMPETITIVE ANALYSIS

This section of the business plan is compiled to evaluate the current and potential competition the business may face when it enters the market with its new plan.

An in-depth analysis of the strengths and weaknesses of your competition is a crucial element of the business plan. Businesses usually make use of a simple process that helps them identify what they are or might be up against when they put this plan into action. You can begin with:

Create a Profile of Your Current Competitors

The first step would be to compile all those businesses that can currently compete against your product/service. To make things simple, focus on the ones that can give you direct competition. For example, continuing with organic soap as our product, you could face competition from:

- Organic soap retailers in your vicinity
- Online businesses selling organic soaps

It is important to note at this point that there isn't much you can do to compete with online businesses unless you plan to sell online and compete solely on the basis of your exceptional customer services, hassle-free dealing, customer relations, and convenient hours.

Identifying your competitors is probably the most challenging part of the entire process, but once you're through with it, things get interesting. Take each of your competition and individually analyze their:

- **Strengths**. What are they better at?
- **Weaknesses**. What are they lacking that you can capitalize on?
- **Strategies**. How are they attracting customers? Can you do better?
- **Objectives**. What are they after? Market share, business growth or something else.

You could use various sources to gather valuable information about your customers. These might include:

- Their business website
- Their marketing material
- Their business/outlet locations
- Their marketing campaigns
- Their social media pages.

Identify Potential Competitors

New competitors keep popping up all the time. While some do not make it far and successful in the industry, others can emerge as a possible threat to your business. You can expect an influx of newbies if you operate in an industry where:

- Profit margins are relatively high
- There are little or no barriers to entry
- There is high demand but low supply
- And the market is continuously growing

It may often be difficult to identify these competitors but a regular check on the market and industry and an effective strategy to deal with them should have you covered. The idea behind including this section in the business plan is to convey to the reader *(usually financial institutions or board of directors)* that you are aware of the existing and potential market contest that the business plan could face and that the company has checks and balances in place or planned to handle them.

A thorough competitive analysis helps you comprehend your competition better in addition to helping you determine the alterations required for your business strategies to surpass the performance of your competitors.

There's a lot you get to learn about your own business plan, strategies, and operations once you're done evaluating your competitors.

Step 8: BUSINESS Development and Design

Next in line are the details of the business design and development plan. The basic purpose of this section is to provide the readers with a comprehensive description of the subject matter's design – in our case it's the design of the organic soap. It may vary from one company to another – it could be a service, or the employee benefits that the company wished to introduce – anything that the business plan is being made for.

Besides the design description, this section will also lay out the plan to chart the development of subject matter from the organization, production, and marketing point of view along with the developmental budget required to set the plan into motion.

Let's look at each of these elements in detail.

Product Development

This part should contain a detailed process of the development of the product/service. You need to provide a mind map for the development teams to work on. It will contain all the technical, managerial, and marketing aspects of the end product so that everyone is aware of what to do and exactly how to do it.

Organizational Development

This section will cover the details of the organizational changes that would be necessary to see the successful execution of the business plan. It will answer questions like:

- *Would the organization need new talent or more hands on board to kick the ball past the goal post?*
- *Is there specific expertise required to see the completion of the project?*
- *Who does what? Who is in charge?*

- *How would the project transition from one department to another?*
- *What processes would be automated? Are there any processes that require manual labor?*

Development Procedures

For this section, you have to clearly identify each separate stage of the procedure and then in order of dependency, align them into a series of tasks and procedures that will ensure an agile and hassle free flow of the whole process.

The Costs and Scheduling

The schedule will basically outline the timeline of the entire process from the beginning to the end when the business starts reaping its benefits. Following our example, this process would require the stages and time frame from sample product till the time the organic soaps are being sold in the market. This schedule will be supported by the corresponding costs of each stage of process.

The Developmental Budget

The developmental budget should consist of the direct and indirect costs that the organization would likely incur in the development of their product/service. These could include:

- Direct materials *(for products only)*
- Direct labor *(for products only)*
- Overheads
- Sales and marketing expenses *(if required)*
- Administrative costs
- Depreciation expenses *(if relevant)*

From the very initial stage of capital investment and research to the completion of the final project, each step needs to be properly defined with expected timelines and the estimated costs that may incur during the process.

Each of these elements would vary in type, structure, and costs – but the plan would provide the company with exactly how they need to work in order to achieve the ultimate goal.

STEP 9: A PLAN FOR OPERATIONS AND MANAGEMENT

In *STEP 5: The Business Overview*, we gave a brief description of the business, its industry, and its history. Step 9 of the business plan would act as an introduction to the key players of the business for the readers.

This is where you go about explaining the organizational structure your business is formed upon and the people who run it. There are two essential sections to this section, regardless of the purpose of this report:

- The organizational structure
- The management

Let's take a look at these elements in detail:

Business Organization

You can have the most solid business plan to achieve the long term goals of the business, but if you don't have the organizational structure to support it – your plan just might go down the drain.

Which is why, this section has been included in the business plan. It is to help lenders/investors/directors evaluate whether the company within its current structure is capable of achieving its targets. For that:

- You should begin by listing down the job positions in the company.
- Next, describe the job responsibilities for each position
- Outline the hierarchy and the chain of command followed within the company.

For business just starting off, this may include the expected organizational structure they wish to achieve. For established businesses, the organizational structure can vary from simple to complex depending on the size of the business. This is also the section where you mention any plans of hiring specialists and experts to support your business plan.

Business Management

This obviously entails the people who run the show for the company. These people may differ depending on the type of organization the business is *(sole proprietor, partnership, or a corporation).*

Ownership

Who owns the business? This is where you mention that. *What type of business are you?*

- A sole proprietor
- A partnership
- Or a corporation

If you're an incorporated business, mention whether you're the C or the S type. Everything else remains the same where you mention:

- Names of the owners
- Type of ownership
- Their involvement in the business

The Management

To make sure you do not miss out on anything in describing the management profile, use this checklist:

- The names of each person in the management
- Their position and responsibilities
- Their education, experience, background
- Their affiliation with non-profit organizations or charities
- Their compensation, benefits, share of profit (if entitled)
- Their employment type
- Their contribution to the company's success.

The Board

Just like you did for the management, if the company is run by a Board of Directors – list them all by name and position in this section. Make sure you mention their experience, education, background, skills, and their significant contributions to the success of your business.

Alternatively, if there isn't a Board of Directors; any Advisory Board or panel of experts should be adequately mentioned just the same.

It is important at this stage to consider the intended users of the business plan and the purpose it is being drafted for. In case your business plan is intended only to get an approval from the Board of Directors, you can take the liberty to keep this section concise. However, if it's intended to lure potential investors and/or lenders, it has to be much more detailed.

STEP 10: THE FINANCES

The last step and possibly the most important one if you're looking for potential investors/loans is the section of finances. It may not be the up-front element of your plan, but it does form the backbone for it.

Financial data compiled in the form of tables, charts, spreadsheets, and formulae is what sums this section up. It is intended to portray the financial condition of the business. A major chunk of this financial data is based on the financial statements. These include three basic elements:

- The cash flow statement
- The income statement
- The balance sheet (statement of affairs)

These three statements together are able to sketch a clear picture of the value of the company and its abilities to meet short term and long term payments. We'll discuss each of these in detail in this chapter.

The Cash Flow Statement

Cash flow statements are used to keep an eye on the cash inflows and outflows of a company over a certain period of time. They could be drawn quarterly, semi-annually, or annually depending on their purpose.

It covers the cash flows from operating, financing, and investing activities of the business and determines whether by the end of the period the business has a net increase or decrease in the cash reserves of the business.

The Income Statement

The income statement compiles all of the business' incomes and expenditures to determine whether the business is making money or not.

Revenues from sales and other income sources are added together to calculate the net income. From this amount the total expenditure incurred by the business over the period is subtracted to reach the bottom line – whether the business is making profit or not.

This statement helps investors/lenders figure out whether the business is earning enough to pay off their operational, administrative, marketing, and other direct expenditures or not.

A projected income statement can predict the impact of the successful implementation of your business plan.

The Balance Sheet
The balance sheet shows the current worth of the business at a particular point in time. For the investors, a balance sheet highlights the assets owned by the company and the liabilities against them.

It helps them evaluate whether the business is in a position to repay its prevailing liabilities with the assets it owns. The balance sheet also lays out the owner's equity invested in the business.

For the business plan, you'd require a current balance sheet and a forecasted one that predicts the changes that the company might benefit from on the successful execution of the business plan.

Other Financial Details
When businesses are looking for options to raise finance, there is a lot more financial detail required apart from the financial statements. These include ratios, comparisons, profitability calculations, leverage details, and other important things that may help a lender/investor to make the informed decision of putting or not putting their money into your business plan.

The financial information gathered can be expressed in various forms. Typically, the financial statements take the form of spreadsheets, whereas other important financial are portrayed using graphs, charts, and other calculations.

Once you're done compiling this section you're essentially through the process of making a business plan. All you need to do now is to bring it all together.

TIE IT ALL UP TOGETHER – THE CONCLUSION

Let's review everything we've learned from this book thus far. We now know that a well drafted business plan is the compass that helps you chart a new course and steer through unexplored territories that may hold the gold for your business. Therefore, whether you are an existing business or one that is just starting out, you need a business plan.

We broke down the entire process into 10 simple steps for better understanding and grip on each element. It's now time to tie them all up together and compile a comprehensive plan that can take your business exactly where you want it to go. Here's what your business plan should look like using our example of organic soaps: (Remember to use complete sentences and give as much detail as possible)

Research and Planning
Planning is crucial. This is why the first three steps of creating a business plan consume the most time and are probably the most difficult.

Step1: Determine Your Business Goals
We decided on the goal to launch a new brand of organic soaps.

Step 2: Recognize the Strengths of Your Business
Our organic soaps are made from natural ingredients, will carry our brand name that is already established and popular among the masses. The highlight of our soap could be a secret ingredient that addresses skin related problems without side effects.

Step 3: Know Your Market
Our target market consists mainly of men and women suffering from skin diseases. Our secondary market is based on people with sensitive skins and those who prefer organic products over other products.

The Business
All about the business and the business plan

Step 4: The Executive Summary
The executive summary is developed to provide the readers a gist of the business plan at a glance.

Step 5: The Business Overview
Everything the readers might be interested in about the business is listed down in this section.

The Product and the Market
The product and how we plan to sell it.

Step 6: The Marketing Plan
The marketing strategies and methods to be used include indirect promotion, promotional events etc. We wish to use competitive pricing to attract customers, and the product will be available for distribution on our website and outlets.

Step 7: Size Up Your Competition – Competitive Analysis
The market possesses stringent competition, but we have effective strategy and ample strengths to overcome it.

Step 8: BUSINESS Development and Design
The process is streamlined for optimizing production and reducing operating costs for higher profit margins.

The Management and Financing
Step 9: A Plan for Operations and Management
The duties have been defined, and the management has the experience and credentials to take up a challenge of this caliber.

Step 10: The Finances
Our financial statements show steady growth with existing products. The projected financial statements and other financial data portray bright prospects after the implementation of the plan. We have sufficient funds to partly finance the project; the remaining could be raised through debt finance.

It is extremely important to keep in mind that irrespective of how meticulously you plan, things wouldn't always go according to plan. There will always be actions that involve some level of risk. It is up to you how you strike back in these situations.

Compiling a proper business plan incorporates strategic planning, thorough market research, an understanding of financial statements, shaping key ideas and effectively communicating them to others. If you take a closer look, these are the very skills required for successfully running a business.

Hence, a business plan is not just limited to giving your business a direction. It also helps you polish your skills to run the business.

Why don't you get started on your business plan right away? It'll take time – probably six months only to get through the first three steps. Don't waste precious time.

> "IF YOU DON'T BUILD YOUR DREAM, SOMEONE WILL HIRE YOU TO HELP BUILD THEIRS" – TONY A. GASKINS JR.

ABOUT THE AUTHOR

This is the first book of "The Entrepreneur's" series by Philipe Bruce. He is currently in the process of developing his next book: *"Not Just Talents"* which is set to discuss how the millennials are revolutionizing the norms of human resource and human capital management in modern day organizations.

Not Just Talents will contain a detailed account of the sustainable strategies businesses can adopt to improve their talent management process through a better understanding of the millennials and their corporate behavior. Check out www.philipebruce.com for more on Philipe's work.

The author would like to make a special mention of his family, friends, and Dr. Mary Goebel-Lundholm to convey his gratitude for their support and encouragement.

P.O.D.S.
Coaching, LLC

www.ingramcontent.com/pod-product-compliance
Lightning Source LLC
Chambersburg PA
CBHW060647030426
42337CB00018B/3489